FRANK LLOYD WRIGHT

America's Master Architect

By Kathryn Smith

ABBEVILLE PRESS | PUBLISHERS

New York London Paris

To the memory of Edgar Kaufmann, jr.

Front cover: Living room of Aline Barnsdall House, Hollyhock House, Hollywood, California, 1916–21
Back cover: Frank Lloyd Wright and apprentices at Taliesin, 1937
Frontispiece: Taliesin, Spring Green, Wisconsin, 1911–59

Editor: Jeffrey Golick
Designer: Molly Shields
Picture Research: Naomi Ben-Shahar
Production Editor: Leslie Bockol
Production Manager: Lou Bilka

First edition
10 9 8 7 6 5 4 3 2 1

Library of Congress Cataloging-in-Publication Data
Smith, Kathryn.
    Frank Lloyd Wright : America's master architect / by Kathryn Smith. — 1st ed.
        p.   cm.
    Includes bibliographical references and index.
    ISBN 0-7892-0287-5
    1. Wright, Frank Lloyd, 1867–1959.   2. Architects—United States—Biography.   I. Title.
    NA737.W7S42   1998
    720'.92—dc20   96-36004
    [B]

CONTENTS

INTRODUCTION: AMERICA'S MASTER ARCHITECT

[I]n this work I think it would be well to see the growth of the idea.

Wright to the Taliesin Fellowship, August 13, 1952

While there is little dispute that Frank Lloyd Wright (1867–1959) is America's greatest architect, there is a general lack of agreement as to the source and the extent of his achievement. His prodigious legacy embraces decorative art, graphic art, houses, public buildings, commercial buildings, and town planning; indeed, everything needed for a total living environment. Wright's philosophy of organic architecture sought unity in every detail, from furniture to freeways. Over his seventy-year career, he explored ideas that began with the American home and expanded to include the relationship between architecture and landscape and, finally, the relationship between architecture and community. As in a symphony, themes in his work develop, repeat, fall away and return again, in rhythmic patterns. Ultimately, Wright's vision was optimistic; he sought a harmonious balance between man, nature, and society.

Wright took inspiration from both the future and the past. His social philosophy, although grounded in Jeffersonian democracy, was outside the mainstream of its day. Pragmatic and idealistic, autocratic and populist, nostalgic and prophetic—it combined an Emersonian view of the moral good of nature with an American trust in self-reliance. It was based on a romantic understanding of complex economic and social forces as the underpinnings for a new society. Within his ideal state, the architect played a dominant role.

To understand Wright's philosophy requires knowledge of his formative experiences. His life began in 1867 in rural Wisconsin shortly after the Civil War. Westward settlement was swiftly transforming the virgin wilderness that was home to Native Americans into an agrarian countryside. With a family background in Unitarianism he absorbed the ideas of the Transcendentalists, especially Ralph Waldo Emerson and Henry David Thoreau.

The notion of the preeminence of nature, gained from both experience and literature, made a vivid impression on the young Wright. After his arrival in Chicago in 1887, he quickly grasped the implications of the Industrial Revolution, both positive and negative, and began to forge a genuinely authentic American architecture, one in contrast to the European historical styles that dominated the times.

After an apprenticeship with the firm of Adler and Sullivan, in 1893 he established his independent practice in Oak Park, Illinois, by turning his attention to the American home. His goal was nothing less than the creation of the beautiful house in every detail. From the building itself to the furniture, carpets, and table linens, everything attracted his scrutiny, even arrangements of flowers and books.

Wright's formative years came to an end at the turn of the century with his development of a new type of American dwelling—the Prairie House—which, from its debut, started an international revolution that continues to reverberate. Suburbia, a unifying decorative scheme, and a reverence for family life merge in the Prairie House to create a building that, although dedicated to conservative values, was a radical departure from precedent due to its open spatial plan. Emanating from a consistent set of principles, the Prairie House nevertheless offered a variety of solutions to fit differing clients, budgets, and sites.

The period 1903–6 is critical. At this time, Wright made a commitment to modern materials, primarily reinforced concrete, with Unity Temple in Oak Park; and he introduced an austere abstraction with the Larkin Administration Building in Buffalo. For the remainder of this period, he continued to produce numerous houses for middle-class families and several on a very grand scale when the client and budget permitted.

Feeling restricted by suburbia both personally and professionally, Wright soon sought a wider context for his expression. Redefining his ambitions in 1911 with the building of a new house and studio, Taliesin, he began an exhaustive search for a language that would reestablish a vital connection between architecture and nature, a link that Wright believed had existed in preliterate cultures.

Where Wright had used representation in the Prairie House, he now chose abstraction. For instance, in the art glass of the earlier Dana House (1902–4) in Springfield, Illinois, crystallized butterflies float over the dining room table as hanging lamps, and light plays against the stylized sumac leaves of the windows as if the house were being caressed by the forest. Taliesin became instead a metaphor for the surrounding landscape. Low roof lines echoed the profile of the hills, the walls were stained the color of the sand of the neighboring Wisconsin River, and native stone was laid up in horizontal layers to recall the stratified rock nearby.

The transition from the elaboration of a decorative style to the creation of a potent symbol of nature was facilitated by Wright's contact with Asian art. He had begun collecting Japanese prints as early as 1902. In 1905, he left the United States for the first time to spend three months in Japan. With information clearly gained in advance from books and

EDGAR J. KAUFMANN HOUSE, FALLINGWATER, Mill Run, Pennsylvania, 1934–37. (ABOVE)

Studio of Kano Motonobu (1476–1559). Detail of **THE FOUR ACCOMPLISHMENTS,** late 16th to early 17th century (Muromachi Period). Ink and color on paper, 65¾ × 101⅜ (167 × 358 cm). (BELOW)

INTERIOR, William Palmer House, Ann Arbor, Michigan, 1950.

AMERICA'S MASTER ARCHITECT

Japanese associates, Wright systematically sought out historic shrines and gardens, Japanese art and craft. By 1916, when he sailed for Japan to spend the majority of the next six years in Tokyo building the Imperial Hotel, he was eager to accumulate not only thousands of wood block prints, but screens, textiles, ceramics, printed papers, bronzes, sculptures, and rugs. Intellectually, these six years were ones of study and reflection, in which Wright found inspiration for many of the themes that would rejuvenate his work between 1925 and 1936. In Asian art, Wright discovered an aesthetic that revealed the inner geometric structure of nature, and which used elements of flora and fauna to symbolize a powerful and meaningful cosmology. His early exposure to and background in Transcendentalism prepared him for these points of view but not for the complex task of translating them into architectural form.

With the Hollyhock House (1916–21) in Hollywood, California, Wright began to refine the elements that would constitute his new domestic vocabulary: earth, fire, water, and the dome of the sky. By the 1920s, with his invention of a concrete block system of construction, he had created the perfect fusion of art and nature. These square concrete blocks, made partly of decomposed granite excavated in situ, were intended for all walls, floors, and even the roof. Structure and ornament, the building and the earth, became one.

In the following years, until his death, Frank Lloyd Wright designed on many levels simultaneously; he would introduce and reintroduce a given architectural idea in building after building until he perfected his composition. At the same time, he initiated new directions and areas of investigation beyond the strict confines of architecture. He was stimulated by the development of a personal aesthetic as well as the changing needs and demands of society. Although he almost always designed as the result of a specific commission from a client, on occasion he would investigate a theoretical problem in a fully worked-out scheme, usually for publication or exhibition. This dual evolution had particular relevance for the period between 1925 and 1936, in which he culminated his exploration of the connection between architecture and nature with the masterful Edgar J. Kaufmann country house, Fallingwater, and began to formulate his ideas for a new social order.

Wright's planning principles were now formed against the backdrop of the Great Depression, which challenged the average American's trust in the status quo. He presented his planning scheme in a model and text that he exhibited at Rockefeller Center in 1935. He called his vision "Broadacre City" to both confuse and confound his critics. Although the low-density zones of his *Usonia* (a term coined to refer to the United States of America) did, indeed, require a minimum of one acre of land per family, the resulting form of the metropolis did not conform to the prevailing definitions of a city. Decentralization, which he predicted would ultimately spread across the entire nation and swallow up all existing urban centers, was made possible by the automobile, telephone, radio, and television. The historical need for vertical density—geographic proximity to work and culture—had been made obsolete by modern transportation and telecommunications. "The city would go to

INTERIOR, Solomon R. Guggenheim Museum, New York, 1943–59.

the country," as Wright predicted, but without the urban congestion that he believed was the root of all economic and social injustice.

Lacking support for his reforms from any government, federal or local, Wright carried out his ideas on a smaller scale with individual clients. He had not forgotten the middle-class families that had formed the core of his practice during the Prairie House period; Broadacre City was to be built one Usonian House at a time. In the period between the Depression and the beginning of World War II, affordable middle-class housing was in short supply and Wright directed his attention to the construction system as well as the plan. The Usonian House formed a "kit of parts," a standard vocabulary of elements for the erection of floors, walls, windows, fireplaces, and roof. It assumed the elimination of the contractor as middle-man between architect and client. It challenged the homeowner to become involved in the construction of his own house. With efficient spaces, judicious proportions, and the elimination of the inessential, it embodied the ideal of "a natural house."

Between the end of World War II and his death in 1959 at the age of ninety-one, Wright would have abundant opportunities to express his views on man, nature, and society; during this period, he received more commissions than at any other stage of his career. The buildings he designed at this time are distinguished by their optimistic mood. The Usonian Automatic method of concrete block construction revived his earlier system of the 1920s for a generation of American veterans returning from the war. Indeed, the postwar housing shortage provided an opportunity to demonstrate the theory that decentralization in a mobile society could provide open space, light, and intimate contact with nature for all Americans.

In the 1950s, Wright's studio was filled with projects for churches, office buildings, schools, hotels, and theaters. The dozens of schemes that he produced for the Solomon R. Guggenheim Museum in New York during the 1940s and 1950s were proof of his continued facility and tenacity. The solid rectangular blocks of the first decades of the century had given way to fluid curves encircling yet not containing space. With the Guggenheim Museum, Wright seems to have attained the promise of his earlier work—a building of continuity and plasticity that was a direct expression of the modern materials that formed it.

Frank Lloyd Wright sought to reconcile many of the opposing forces of the twentieth century: the rationalism of the machine with the mysteries of the earth, the rights of the individual with the need for community. Although Wright was a futurist, he dedicated his cause to traditional architectural values. The very paradoxes and contradictions that make him so difficult to compartmentalize are what give him such lasting appeal. His aesthetic prowess is unchallenged: masterpieces such as Fallingwater, Unity Temple, the Robie House, the Guggenheim Museum, and many more are among the greatest architectural landmarks in the United States, and possibly the world. At an early age Wright announced that his ambition was to become not only the greatest architect of his generation, but the greatest architect that ever lived. It is too early to render a judgment, but there is no doubt that his legacy will continue to influence generations well into the next century.

FORMATIVE YEARS (1887–1899)

Good friend, around these hearth-stones speak no evil word of any creature.

Inscribed over the mantel, Frank Lloyd Wright House & Studio

In 1887, when Frank Lloyd Wright was not yet twenty-one, he decided to leave his hometown, Madison, Wisconsin, and move to Chicago to become an architect. Within a short time he began work with the firm of Adler and Sullivan, which had earned a well-deserved reputation for the design of tall commercial buildings. Louis Sullivan recognized Wright's talent and eventually made him his assistant. Even at this early stage of his career Wright exhibited a predilection for residential architecture, and he began to design the few domestic commissions that Adler and Sullivan accepted.

With his marriage in 1889 to Catherine Lee Tobin and the birth of six children following in quick succession from 1890 to 1903, Wright built and then repeatedly remodeled his own house in the suburb of Oak Park. It was here that he perfected many of his ideas for the American family dwelling: the pinwheel plan that rotates around a masonry hearth as the gathering place for family and friends, the spacious dining room with a table enclosed by high-backed chairs lit by an indirect electric light fixture overhead, the playroom reserved for entertainment, whether intimate and casual, or festive and formal.

With a few notable exceptions, especially the plan for Chicago's Wolf Lake Amusement Park (1895), Wright's independent practice that began in 1893 was devoted to domesticity. Both in his home life and professional life, Wright dedicated himself to the complete redefinition of the American house. He seems to have been guided by the views of William C. Gannett, a family friend and the author of *The House Beautiful* (1895). (Wright designed and hand-printed an edition of the book in 1897 in partnership with his first independent client, William H. Winslow [see page 21].) Gannett discusses the importance not only of the careful selection and arrangement of the physical elements of a house—its architecture, furnishings, and decoration—but also how these elements create "The Building of God, not made with Hands." He emphasizes the spiritual life of the residents based on a reverence for familial values: consideration, love, and union.

During the 1890s, Wright executed several houses where the building appears to hug the ground, due to strong horizontal lines and a deep pitch to the roof. He experimented with the plan, opening the interior to create a more generous flow of space. He simplified the plan with built-in furniture—cabinetry and seating—and designed his own chairs and tables using unpainted wood, which was then simply stained and waxed. In sympathy with the principles of the Arts and Crafts movement, he rejected the cluttered surfaces of the Victorian house and designed simple vessels to hold arrangements of weeds or wildflowers cut from a nearby roadside.

In 1898, he added a studio to his house in Oak Park (pages 24–25) so that he could be closer to his work. The top-lit, two-story drafting room and intimate octagonal library housed a small staff of draftsmen and secretaries. With his own house as his best form of advertising, Wright began to attract clients from Oak Park and the neighboring suburb of River Forest. By 1900, he had something of historic significance to offer them.

LIVING ROOM, Frank Lloyd Wright House, Oak Park, Illinois, 1889–90. (PAGE 14)

WILLIAM H. WINSLOW HOUSE, River Forest, Illinois, 1893–94. (LEFT)

INGLENOOK, William H. Winslow House, 1893–94. (BELOW)

For Dankmar Adler (1844–1900) and Louis Sullivan (1856–1924), **CHARNLEY-PERSKY HOUSE,** Chicago, 1891–92.

DINING ROOM, Frank Lloyd Wright
House, 1895.

FRANK LLOYD WRIGHT HOUSE, Oak Park, Illinois, 1889–90.

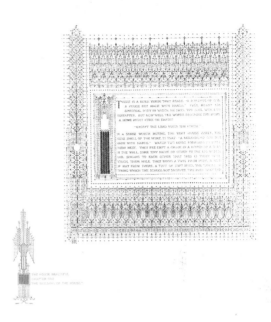

Frank Lloyd Wright and family on the steps of his Oak Park house, c. 1890. Wright is seated at right; at center Catherine Wright holds their child, Lloyd. (ABOVE)

PLAYROOM, Frank Lloyd Wright House, 1895. (LEFT)

WEED HOLDERS, c. 1895. Copper, each 28 × 4¼ × 4¼ in.(71.1 × 11.4 × 11.4 cm).

URN, c. 1895. Copper and galvanized tin, 17½ × 17½ in. (44.5 × 44.5 cm).

PRAIRIE PERIOD (1900–1910)

Now what can be eliminated?

Wright, ARCHITECTURAL FORUM, January 1938

ABOVE)

By 1900 Frank Lloyd Wright had created a new type of single family dwelling that he believed was the direct result of the changed circumstances of modern living. The Prairie House appealed to a progressive segment of Chicago's middle class because it represented a practical, new way of life—full of "light, air, and prospect"—in contrast to the claustrophobic, cluttered rooms of the Victorian house. The spatial innovation of the plan—the public rooms open to each other on the diagonal creating an open floor plan—was made feasible by the invention of modern mechanical heating systems. Wright eliminated the compartmentalization of the traditional house, the boxes within a box, allowing fluid movement where walls begin to define, rather than enclose, space. This was the first revolutionary change in architectural space since the Renaissance, and a younger generation of European architects and designers such as Mies van der Rohe and Theo van Doesburg seized on the discovery when Wright's work was published in Germany shortly before World War I.

The Prairie Houses, so named because their horizontal lines imitated the flat ground plane so common throughout the Midwest, had a T-shape plan with a central masonry chimney; later, the plan developed variations, but the spatial flow around the fireplace at the core remained a common element. The interiors responded to family life. Despite innovations in heating, Wright emphasized the symbolic importance of the hearth as a gathering place for the family. Seating was comprised of either built-in or freestanding pieces grouped around the fireplace. A spacious dining room ritualized meals. Wright created a room within a room with the addition of

a custom-designed dining table and high-backed chairs. Despite its common features, the architect believed that there should be as many different Prairie Houses as there were people, each a unique creation specifically suited to the particulars of the time, the place, and the client.

While the Prairie House demonstrated Wright's ability to perfect a domestic style, the opportunity to design public buildings between 1903 and 1906 ushered in a rigorous abstraction more attuned to the spirit of the industrial age. The solid rectangular block of the Larkin Administration Building in Buffalo, New York (page 35), was relieved at the corners by slender vertical stair towers. Inside, the interior light court was top-lit, each floor ringed with a high band of windows and built-in filing cabinets, with metal office furniture designed to make cleaning efficient. The cubic severity of Unity Temple in Oak Park, Illinois (pages 38–39), is accomplished through the uncompromising use of exposed reinforced concrete on the exterior. With the boldly expressed precision of the two cubes—one for the congregation, the other for meeting rooms—and the austerity of the material, Unity Temple was Wright's most daring contribution to the machine age.

The abstraction of the early work can be interpreted as the search for an architectural language for the twentieth century, an attempt at transforming industrial materials into monumental architectural form, and a clear statement about the potential of modern construction methods. The commissions that Wright received between 1903 and 1906 stimulated these concerns and laid a foundation for their development in the years ahead.

HANGING LAMP (BUTTERFLY LAMP), Susan
Lawrence Dana House, 1902–4. Leaded glass,
19 × 23½ × 23½ in. (48.2 × 59.7 × 59.7 cm).
(ABOVE)

Oak Park,

win D.
York,
scent, and
39¾ ×
AGE 28)

DINING ROOM, Susan Lawrence Dana House, 1902–4. (ABOVE)

WINDOW, Susan Lawrence Dana House, 1902–4. Leaded glass and wood frame, 46¼ × 31½ in.
(117.5 × 80 cm). (LEFT)

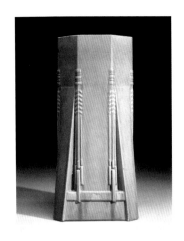

TECO VASE, Susan Lawrence Dana House, c. 1902–4. Glazed earthenware, height: 23⅜ in. (59.4 cm).

SUSAN LAWRENCE DANA HOUSE, Springfield, Illinois, 1902–4. (BELOW)

MAIN FLOOR, Larkin Administration Building, 1902–6.

OFFICE CHAIR, Larkin Administration
Building, 1902–6. Painted steel with
leather-covered seat and casters, 38 ×
24½ × 21 in. (96.5 × 61.6 × 53.3 cm).
(ABOVE LEFT)

EXECUTIVE OFFICE, Larkin Administration
Building, 1902–6. (ABOVE RIGHT)

LARKIN ADMINISTRATION BUILDING,
Buffalo, New York, 1902–6; demolished
1950. (LEFT)

THOMAS P. HARDY HOUSE, Racine, Wisconsin, 1905. Perspective. (ABOVE)

EDWIN H. CHENEY HOUSE, Oak Park, Illinois, 1903. Perspective. (BELOW)

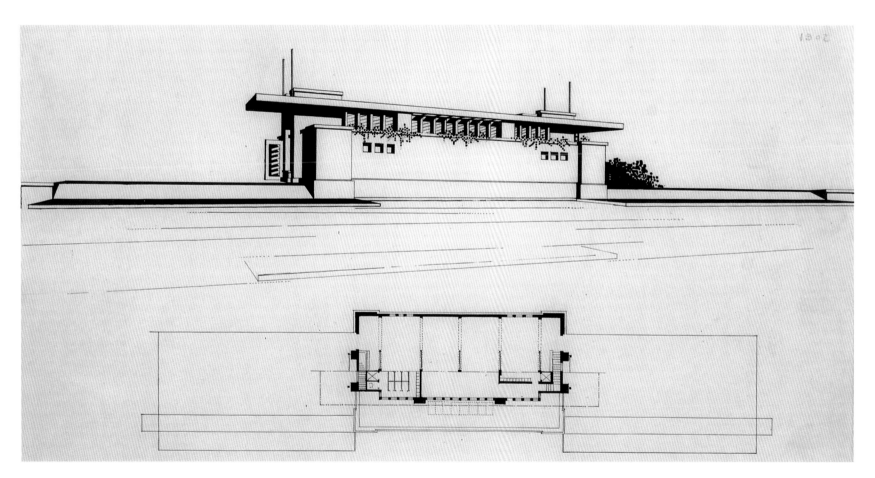

YAHARA BOATHOUSE, Madison, Wisconsin, 1905; unbuilt. Perspective.

INTERIOR, Unity Temple, 1905–8. (OPPOSITE)

LIGHT FIXTURE, Unity Temple, 1905–8. (LEFT)

UNITY TEMPLE, Oak Park, Illinois, 1905–8. Perspective. (BELOW)

SIDE CHAIR, c. 1904. Oak with leather-covered seat, 39¼ × 15 × 19¼ in. (99.6 × 38 × 48.9 cm). (ABOVE)

SIDE CHAIR, Raymond W. Evans House, Chicago, 1908. Oak, height: 44¾ in. (114 cm). (RIGHT)

Frank Lloyd Wright (left) and family on the porch of his Oak Park House, 1903. Photograph by Frank Lloyd Wright.

SCONCE, Avery Coonley House, 1908. Bronze, frosted glass globe, mica,
7¼ × 11 × 9 in. (18.4 × 28 × 22.8 cm). (LEFT)

CHAIRS, Avery Coonley House, 1908. Oak with leather-covered seat, height
(l to r): 36 in. (91.4 cm), 40⅛ in. (100.2 cm), 37 in. (94 cm). (BELOW)

AVERY COONLEY HOUSE, Riverside, Illinois, 1906–8.

COPPER FRIEZE,
Meyer May House,
1908.

MURAL, Meyer May House, 1908. (ABOVE LEFT)

MEYER MAY HOUSE, Grand Rapids, Michigan, 1908. (ABOVE)

LIVING ROOM WINDOWS, Meyer May House, 1908. (LEFT)

LIVING ROOM, Meyer May House, 1908.

LIVING ROOM DETAIL, Meyer May
House, 1908.

CHILD'S BEDROOM, Meyer May House, 1908.
(ABOVE)

DINING ROOM, Meyer May House, 1908. (LEFT)

LIVING ROOM, Frederick C. Robie House, 1908–10. (ABOVE)

FREDERICK C. ROBIE HOUSE, Chicago, 1908–10. (OPPOSITE)

FIREPLACE, Frederick C. Robie House, 1908–10. (OPPOSITE)

FRENCH DOORS, Frederick C. Robie House, 1908–10. (BELOW)

MRS. THOMAS GALE HOUSE, Oak Park, Illinois, 1909. Perspective.

DR. GEORGE C. STOCKMAN HOUSE, Mason City, Iowa, 1908.

JAPAN AND CALIFORNIA (1911-1924)

There should lie in the very science and poetry of structure
the inspired love of Nature.

Wright, A TESTAMENT, 1957

Throughout the 1900s Frank Lloyd Wright's commitment to domestic architecture reflected his own personal circumstances. By 1911, he had separated from his wife and children and built a rural retreat, Taliesin (Welsh for "shining brow") (pages 56–57), in the countryside of Wisconsin. The implications of this exodus from suburbia would resonate in Wright's thinking for the next two and a half decades. Taliesin, made up of three wings containing house, studio, and farm, was built into a gently sloping hillside bordering land settled by Wright's Welsh grandparents and maternal aunts and uncles. The design reflected years of contemplation on the unique character of the site. Seen from a distance, Taliesin rises from the hillside like a stratified cliff echoing the profile of the low-lying hills across the horizon. Natural references—walls built up of rough-hewn limestone mimicking local rock outcroppings, and plaster stained the warm color of the banks of the nearby Wisconsin River—are unmistakable.

While it was a masterful demonstration of Wright's ideas about the transcendent relation between architecture and landscape, Taliesin was not prophetic of the work of the following decade. Between 1911 and 1924 Wright had few opportunities to explore these themes further because he had little work. It is ironic that Wright's next monumental public building was built so far from his new home.

Japan, the destination of an earlier intellectual odyssey, welcomed him with the commission for a new Western-style hotel. Wright's preoccupation with the Imperial Hotel (pages 66–67) for six years, between 1916 and 1922, resulted in a period of languishing productivity back in the United States,

where a flourishing practice eluded him. In the end, the hotel provoked ambivalence. Its technological advances, such as the reinforced concrete frame and experimental structural foundation, received praise. Its massive and ornate decorative scheme with decided overtones of primitivism antagonized those critics who were then embracing the machine-age architecture of Europe.

In 1923, shortly after his return to the United States, Wright ingeniously seized upon the idea of standardization as a means to harmonize mechanization and nature, when he invented the textile block system of concrete construction. A 16-inch-square unit was manufactured from cement and decomposed granite excavated from the building site. When laid end upon end, row upon row, the blocks formed cylindrical hollows along their edges through which slender rods of steel were inserted. Next, liquid concrete was poured into the channels and when dried, the blocks formed a monolithic wall. With one stroke, Wright had created a standardized unit that was at once modular, structural, functional, ornamental, and a direct link to the earth from which the building rose.

In 1923 Wright relocated to Los Angeles where he hoped to build large projects with his new system. He excited some interest in his invention among the real estate speculators of California. In the end, however, only four houses were built: Millard (page 70), Storer (opposite and page 71), Ennis (page 72), and Freeman (page 73). Disenchanted, but not discouraged, Wright returned to Taliesin in 1924.

FRANK LLOYD WRIGHT'S
BEDROOM, Taliesin,
1911–59. (RIGHT)

LIVING ROOM, John Storer
House, Hollywood,
California, 1923–24.
(PAGE 54)

TALIESIN, Spring Green, Wisconsin, 1911–59. (ABOVE)

LIVING ROOM AND DINING ALCOVE, Taliesin, 1911–59. (LEFT)

AVERY COONLEY PLAYHOUSE, Riverside, Illinois, 1912. (LEFT)

WINDOWS, Avery Coonley Playhouse, 1912. Leaded glass, 40½ × 64½ in. (102.7 × 165 cm). (BELOW)

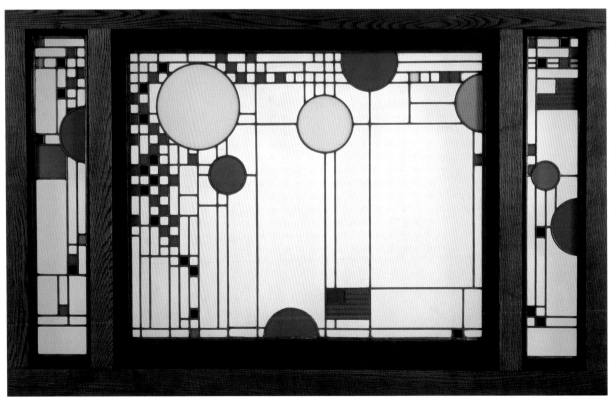

INTERIOR, Avery Coonley Playhouse, 1912.

MIDWAY GARDENS, Chicago, 1913–14; demolished 1929. Perspective. (BELOW)

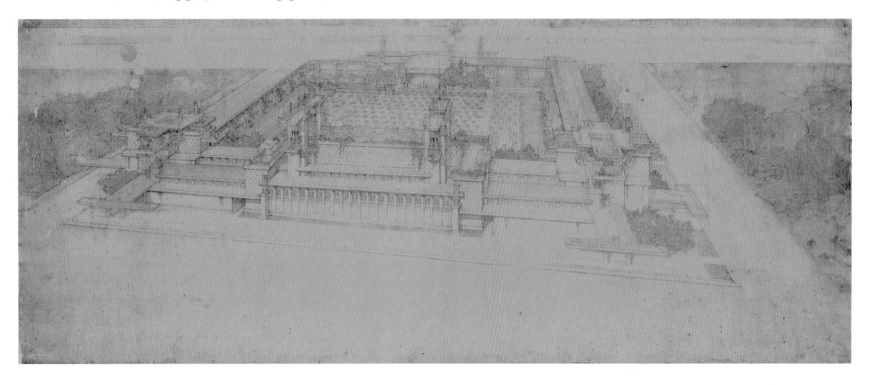

SUMMER GARDEN, Midway Gardens, 1913–14. (OPPOSITE)

Frank Lloyd Wright,
c. 1910–20.

SPRITE, Midway Gardens, 1913–14. (RIGHT)

AMERICAN SYSTEM-BUILT HOUSES FOR THE RICHARDS COMPANY, 1915–17. Perspective of model c3 (AR). Lithoprint, 11 × 8½ in. (27.9 × 21.6 cm). (RIGHT)

FRANCIS W. LITTLE HOUSE, NORTHOME, Deephaven, Minnesota, 1912–14, Living Room; demolished 1972. Living room reconstructed 1982 at The Metropolitan Museum of Art. (OPPOSITE)

AMERICAN·MODEL·C3 □ ·PATENTS□□
·APPLIED·FOR
AMERICAN·SYSTEM-BUILT
HOUSES □ DESIGNED·BY
FRANK·LLOYD·WRIGHT■
THE·RICHARDS·COMPANY
PROPRIETORS·MILWAUKEE

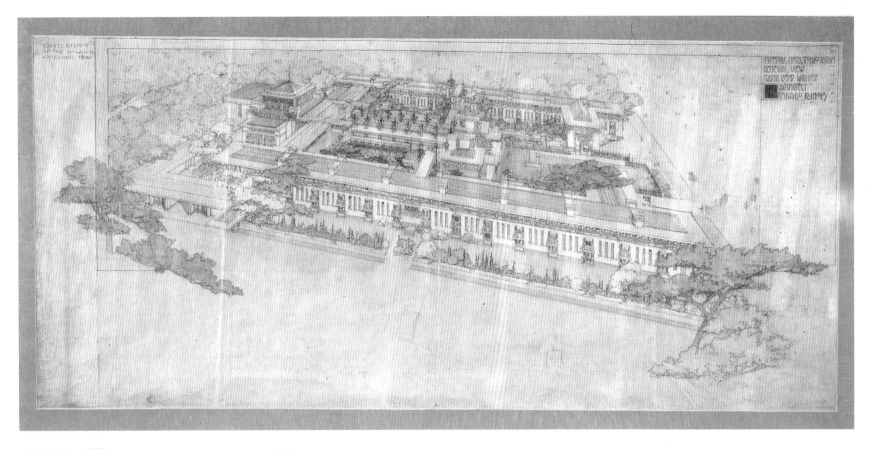

IMPERIAL HOTEL, Tokyo, 1913–23; demolished 1968. Perspective. (ABOVE)

TEA SERVICE, Imperial Hotel, 1913–23. (LEFT)

FIREPLACE, Imperial Hotel, 1913–23. (OPPOSITE)

LIVING ROOM, Aline Barnsdall House, 1916–21. (LEFT)

ALINE BARNSDALL HOUSE, HOLLYHOCK HOUSE,
Hollywood, California, 1916–21. (OPPOSITE)

DINING ROOM, Aline Barnsdall House, 1916–21. (RIGHT)

JOHN STORER HOUSE, Hollywood, California, 1923–24. (ABOVE)

ALICE MILLARD HOUSE, LA MINIATURA, Pasadena, California, 1923–24. (OPPOSITE)

CONCRETE BLOCK, Ennis-Brown House, 1924–25. (LEFT)

ENNIS-BROWN HOUSE, Hollywood, California, 1924–25. (BELOW)

CORNER WINDOW, Samuel Freeman House, 1924–25. (ABOVE)

SAMUEL FREEMAN HOUSE, Hollywood, California, 1924–25. (LEFT)

REGENERATION AND RENEWAL (1925-1936)

The good building makes the landscape more beautiful
than it was before the building was built.

Wright, "Two Lectures on Architecture," 1931

If the years 1911–24 marked a transition, they were followed by a period of invention from 1925–36 when Frank Lloyd Wright generated many of the ideas and elements that would form the foundation for his late work. While he struggled to support himself and his family with whatever jobs came his way, he was producing original architectural compositions and formulating a vision for a radical utopian society.

Since few commissions of this period were built, Wright was forced to put these drawings aside until opportunity presented itself later. Out of the plan for the Gordon Strong Automobile Objective (1924–25, page 77), for example, the spiral ramp of the Guggenheim Museum (1943–59, page 124) was born. The National Life Insurance Building (1924–25) and St. Mark's-in-the-Bouwerie Towers (1927–31, both page 76) use Wright's principles of cantilever construction for their towers. Likening a skyscraper to a tree, Wright proposed to project the floors of the building from the structural core like branches from a trunk. Decades later, the Johnson Research Laboratory Tower (1943–50, page 105) and Price Tower (1952–56, page 119) would both employ this idea.

Although Wright had returned to the Midwest, many of his commissions were located in wilderness areas of the United States, presenting him with vistas of unparalleled natural beauty. Whether on a mountain top in Maryland for the Gordon Strong Automobile Objective or in the harsh Arizona desert with the San Marcos-in-the-Desert Resort Hotel (1928–29) (page 77), Wright sought a sublime connection between the building and the pristine landscape around it.

Returning to the theme that he had inaugurated with the design of Taliesin, Wright pursued devices and motifs throughout these years to ground architecture visually and symbolically in nature. He reached the apotheosis of his search with the design for the Edgar J. Kaufmann country house, Fallingwater (pages 82–85). By placing the house over waterfalls, Wright guaranteed that architecture and nature would form one consummate union rather than a composition of disparate parts. He further reinforced the relationship by mimicking the form and arrangement of the waterfalls in the building—the broad concrete terraces echo the rock ledges below. While the building differentiates itself from its surroundings and retains its identity as a man-made object, it is perceived as a complement to nature; and as a result, each ennobles the other by its presence.

During these years, Wright was formulating a new strain of thought as a result of the turbulent economic and political conditions brought on by the Great Depression. He couched his reform in terms of town planning and called his ideal community Broadacre City (page 81). He first summarized his ideas in a book, *The Disappearing City*, which appeared in 1932, and again in *When Democracy Builds*, published in 1945. Broadacre City was based on the principle of decentralization and assumed that the nation would be crisscrossed by great arterial highways. It called for a pattern of low density settlement across the American landscape that would allow every family a minimum of one acre of land, one automobile, and access to telecommunications. Without government support, Wright was reduced to seeing his ideas realized on a small scale with individual clients as scores of middle-class Americans turned to him again as the country recovered from the Depression.

NATIONAL LIFE INSURANCE COMPANY BUILDING, Chicago, 1924–25; unbuilt. Perspective. (ABOVE)

ST. MARK'S-IN-THE-BOUWERIE TOWERS, New York, 1927–31; unbuilt. Perspective. (RIGHT)

EDGAR J. KAUFMANN HOUSE, FALLINGWATER, Mill Run, Pennsylvania, 1934–37. (PAGE 74)

GORDON STRONG AUTOMOBILE
OBJECTIVE, Sugarloaf Mountain,
Maryland, 1924–25; unbuilt.
Perspective. (LEFT)

SAN MARCOS-IN-THE-DESERT RESORT, Chandler, Arizona, 1928–29; unbuilt. Perspective. (BELOW)

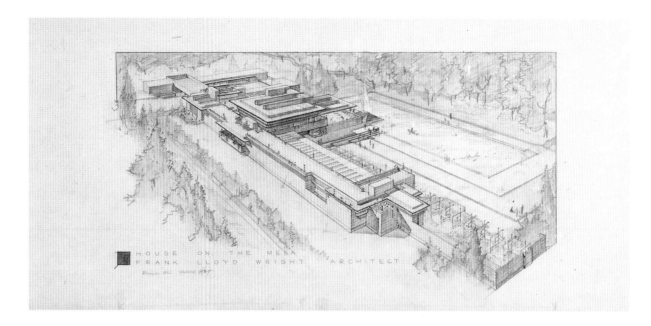

HOUSE ON THE MESA, Denver, Colorado, 1931; unbuilt. Perspective. (RIGHT)

RICHARD LLOYD JONES HOUSE, WESTHOPE, Tulsa, Oklahoma, 1928–31. (BELOW)

SAN MARCOS-IN-THE-DESERT RESORT, Chandler, Arizona, 1928–29; unbuilt. Perspective. (BELOW)

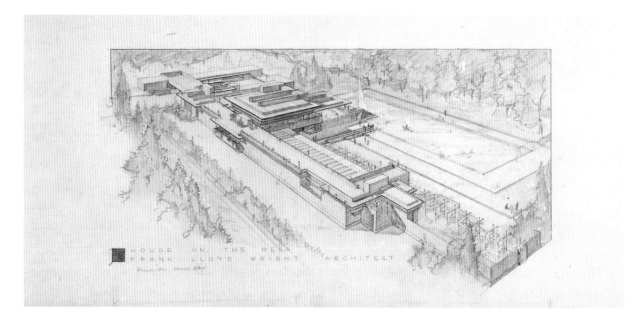

HOUSE ON THE MESA, Denver, Colorado, 1931; unbuilt. Perspective. (RIGHT)

RICHARD LLOYD JONES HOUSE, WESTHOPE, Tulsa, Oklahoma, 1928–31. (BELOW)

RICHARD LLOYD JONES HOUSE, WESTHOPE, 1928–31.

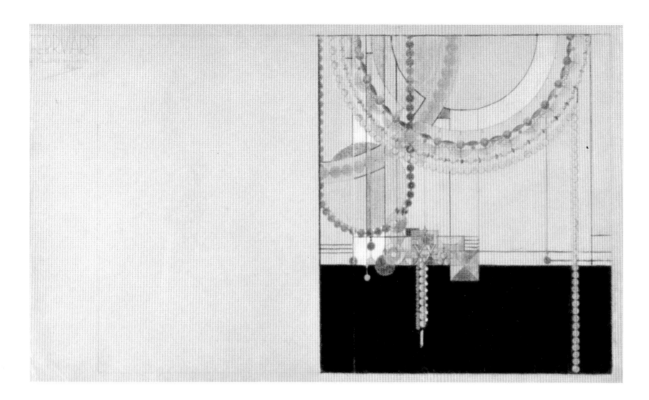

FEBRUARY, LIBERTY Magazine Cover, c. 1927. Pencil and crayon on paper, 14¼ × 24 in. (36.2 × 60.1 cm). (LEFT)

APRIL, LIBERTY Magazine Cover, c. 1927. Pencil and crayon on paper, 14⅛ × 24 in. (35.9 × 60.1 cm). (RIGHT)

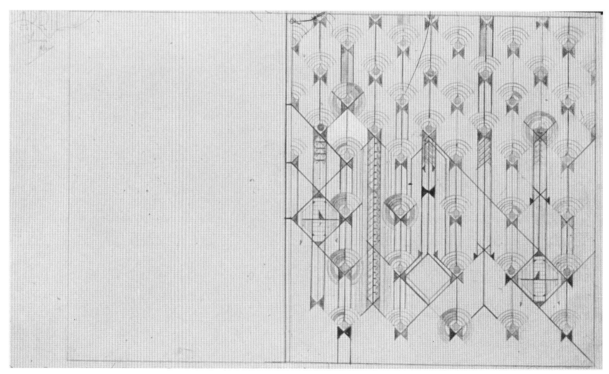

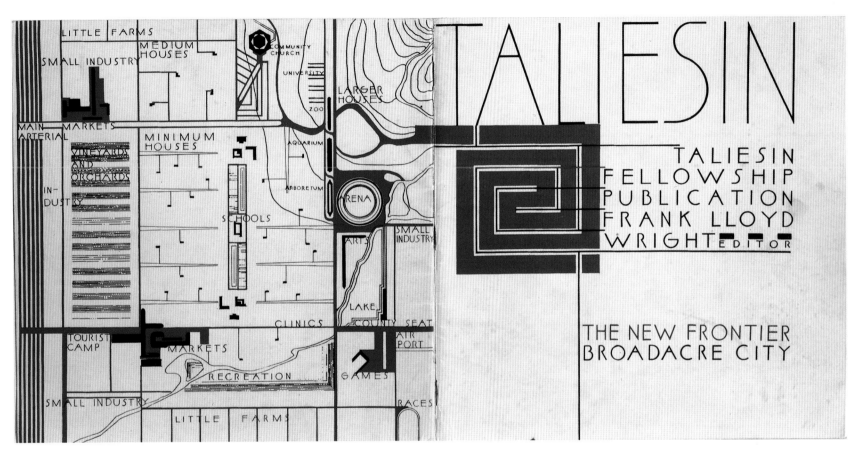

BROADACRE CITY, 1932, plan.

EDGAR J. KAUFMANN HOUSE, FALLINGWATER, 1934–37. (ABOVE)

EDGAR J. KAUFMANN HOUSE, FALLINGWATER, Mill Run, Pennsylvania, 1934–37. (OPPOSITE)

HATCH, Edgar J. Kaufmann House, 1934–37.

FIREPLACE, Edgar J. Kaufmann House, 1934–37.

LIVING ROOM, Edgar J. Kaufmann House, 1934–37. (OPPOSITE)

INTERIOR, S. C. Johnson & Son Administration Building, 1936–39. (ABOVE)

ADVERTISING DEPARTMENT RECEPTION DESK, S. C. Johnson & Son
   Administration Building, 1936–39. (RIGHT)

S. C. JOHNSON & SON ADMINISTRATION BUILDING, Racine, Wisconsin,
   1936–39. (OPPOSITE)

USONIAN PERIOD (1937-1947)

This Usonian dwelling seems a thing loving the ground with a new sense of space, light, and freedom—to which our U.S.A. is entitled.

Wright, THE NATURAL HOUSE, 1954

From the late 1930s until the beginning of World War II, Wright produced numerous regional variations of a housing type for his *Usonia* (a word coined to refer to the United States of America). In 1936, after several years of preliminary studies, he committed himself to designing and building a Usonian House for Herbert and Katherine Jacobs (opposite) for five thousand dollars. The one-story house with a flat roof opened to a generous private garden through a wall of French doors while turning a solid back to the street. The compact L-shaped plan contained two wings (one for the living room and dining alcove, the other for bedrooms and study), with the kitchen and one bath at the hinge of the L. To lower costs even further, Wright eliminated the garage by substituting an innovation: a covered but open shelter called a carport.

He believed the construction system was the source of high cost in housing. Along with glass, he used a few essential materials—concrete, brick, and wood—left unfinished or simply stained or waxed. He eliminated an excavated basement by pouring a concrete slab as foundation and finished floor. Brick piers and fireplaces were erected to be followed by construction of a sandwich wall of wood boards and batten, the same on the exterior and interior. The flat roof, windows and doors completed the structure. The total cost included built-in seating, tables, bookshelves, cabinets, and lighting.

The design reflected Wright's awareness of the changing nature of the American family. The spatial layout assumed the absence of servants, the importance of the housewife supervising the children, and an informal social life with time spent relaxing in the garden. Although the early Usonian Houses were designed for typical rectangular suburban lots, as the years went by Wright became increasingly impatient with the cramped spaces and pretentious houses of suburbia and he urged his prospective clients to buy one acre plots out in the country. He then introduced variations in plan to provide optimum orientation toward the sun, and to best accommodate the topography of the site, including vistas of natural features such as lakes or mountains.

Wright was unable to carry out his vision of Broadacre City, given the economic and political reforms it required. As a result, he welcomed opportunities to extend the benefits of *Usonia*—open space, light, and direct contact with nature—to an increasingly mobile society. Usonian Houses were built in every region of the United States and, whether in Arizona or Alabama, Wright used indigenous materials to anchor the building to its native locale.

Government restrictions on materials affected his practice during World War II; but, on turning eighty, he showed no signs of slowing down, or diminished abilities. Indeed, he was approaching his most productive decade. He amply demonstrated his mastery of monumental public buildings, whether in urban or rural settings, in two unbuilt projects: the Pittsburgh Point Civic Center (page 111) and, for Huntington Hartford, several structures designed for a canyon in Hollywood, California (page 110). When the postwar building boom came, it found him ready and eager to take on larger commissions.

HERBERT JACOBS HOUSE, Madison, Wisconsin, 1936–37. (PAGE 88)

COVER, TOWN AND COUNTRY Magazine, 1937. Ink on paper, 13½ × 9¾ in. (34.3 × 24.7 cm). (LEFT)

LIVING ROOM, Paul R. Hanna House, 1935–37. (BELOW)

PAUL R. HANNA HOUSE, HONEYCOMB HOUSE, Palo Alto, California, 1935–37.

HERBERT F. JOHNSON HOUSE,
WINGSPREAD, Racine, Wisconsin,
1937–39.

INTERIOR, Herbert F. Johnson House, 1937–39. (RIGHT)

Frank Lloyd Wright with model of **WINGSPREAD,** c. 1937. (BELOW)

TALIESIN WEST, Scottsdale, Arizona, 1937–59. (ABOVE)

Frank Lloyd Wright and apprentices at Taliesin, 1937. (RIGHT)

| USONIAN PERIOD

GARDEN ROOM, Taliesin West, 1937–59. (ABOVE)

DRAFTING ROOM, Taliesin West, 1937–59. (LEFT)

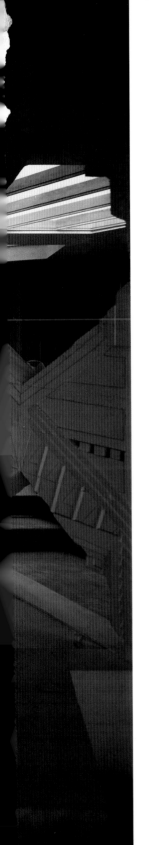

INTERIOR, Annie Pfeiffer Chapel, Florida Southern College, 1938–41. (OPPOSITE)

ANNIE PFEIFFER CHAPEL, FLORIDA SOUTHERN COLLEGE, Lakeland, Florida, 1938–41. (BELOW)

INTERIOR, John C. Pew House, 1938–40. (ABOVE)

JOHN C. PEW HOUSE, Madison, Wisconsin, 1938–40. (RIGHT)

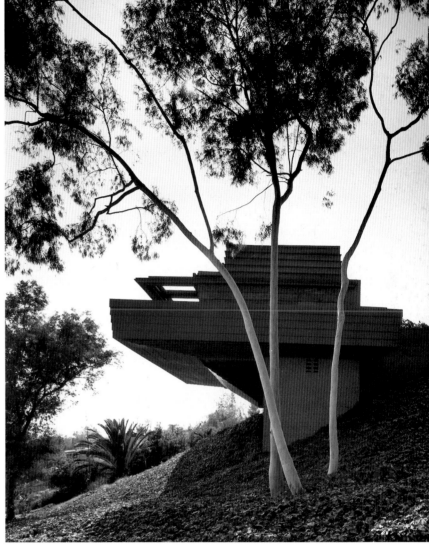

GEORGE D. STURGES HOUSE, Los Angeles, 1939. (ABOVE)

INTERIOR, Georges D. Sturges House, 1939. (LEFT)

MONONA TERRACE CIVIC CENTER, Madison, Wisconsin, 1938; unbuilt. Perspective.

CRYSTAL HEIGHTS HOTEL, SHOPS, AND THEATER, Washington, D.C., 1939; unbuilt. Perspective.

POPE-LEIGHEY HOUSE, Falls Church, Virginia, 1939; relocated 1964 to Mount Vernon, Virginia. (LEFT)

LIVING-DINING AREA, Pope-Leighey House, 1939. (BELOW)

GOETSCH-WINKLER HOUSE, Okemos, Michigan, 1939. (LEFT)

INTERIOR, Goetsch-Winkler House, 1939. (BELOW)

INTERIOR, Herbert Jacobs House, 1943–48. (ABOVE)

HERBERT JACOBS HOUSE, SOLAR HEMICYCLE,
Middleton, Wisconsin, 1943–48. (RIGHT)

INTERIOR, Lowell Walter House, 1945. (ABOVE)

LOWELL WALTER HOUSE, Quasqueton, Iowa, 1945. (RIGHT)

ROGERS LACY HOTEL, Dallas, Texas, 1946–47; unbuilt. Perspective. (BELOW)

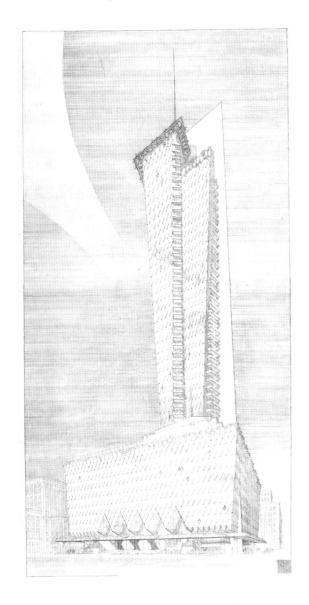

INTERIOR, Melvyn Smith House, 1946. (ABOVE)

MELVYN SMITH HOUSE, Bloomfield Hills, Michigan, 1946.

HUNTINGTON HARTFORD SPORTS CLUB,
Hollywood, California, 1946–48; unbuilt.
Perspective. (ABOVE)

HUNTINGTON HARTFORD HOUSE, Hollywood,
California, 1946–48; unbuilt. Perspective.
(RIGHT)

PITTSBURGH POINT CIVIC CENTER, 1947–48; unbuilt. Perspective.

AQUARIUM, Pittsburgh Point Civic Center, 1947–48; unbuilt. Cutaway Perspective.

LATE WORKS (1948-1959)

When we begin to build buildings that have [an] expression of beauty, of our own time, then we will have an architecture that we can call organic.

Wright to the Taliesin Fellowship, January 30, 1955

As America entered the space age, Frank Lloyd Wright, born two years after the end of the Civil War, had lived long enough to reap the rewards of professional recognition. Honorary degrees, medals, touring exhibitions, magazine covers, and television interviews were bestowed upon him with regularity. He seemed to relish the fame as it brought with it a new audience for his ideas on decentralization, the natural house, and the potential for prefabrication and man-made materials.

At the end, as at the beginning, timing was important. Wright grasped the implications of the postwar building boom and reacted with a burst of energy and creativity. He was discovered by a new generation: returning war veterans in need of housing. He responded by significantly improving the textile block system of concrete construction of the 1920s with a set of guidelines and plans for the do-it-yourself movement.

In order to reduce costs, he proposed eliminating the expense of a contractor and skilled trade workers by using standardized elements that could be made by the homeowner. He made the blocks lighter and simpler to manufacture by changing the shape from square to rectangular and by eliminating ornamental pattern in favor of plain blocks that were either solid or open. In the early 1950s, he received commissions that allowed him to put his theory of Usonian Automatic concrete block construction to the test. Several large houses can be considered impressive demonstrations of the techniques of the system, but their generous budgets do not qualify them as affordable family housing. In the smaller houses where the homeowners participated in construction, some found the complex and time-consuming fabrication was anything but "automatic"; ultimately, however, years after the memories of the building process had faded, they declared that the results proved worth the effort.

More than anything, postwar conditions provided Wright with serious opportunities and proven technology to exercise his virtuosity for public buildings. The Unitarian Church (1945–51, pages 114–15), Beth Sholom Synagogue (1953–59, pages 120–21), and the Annunciation Greek Orthodox Church (1955–61, page 112) pushed the limits on materials and methods while creating modern forms for ancient rituals. Unwilling to allow the Price Tower to go down in history as his final statement on the skyscraper, in 1956 he designed the Mile High Illinois (page 123), a structure of 528 stories for a site overlooking Lake Michigan in Chicago. He fantasized that visitors could ascend to the top of his proposed state office building one mile above ground by a series of atomic-powered elevators. It was ironic that when he received his first commission for a government building, the Marin County Civic Center, it was in California, far from the Midwest that had been the model for his ideal state.

Even more ironic was the fact that his crowning achievement, the Guggenheim Museum (1943–59), would be built in New York City, the focus of his diatribes against urban density. Yet this building conveyed a sculptural weight, a facility with light and space, a virtuosity with the malleable material of concrete, and a dynamic energy that summarized, if not surpassed, earlier masterworks. Although controversial as an exhibition space for modern painting and sculpture, and awkward in many of its details (some attributable to Wright, others to insensitive changes by the owners), it is, unarguably, one of the finest public rooms in the world.

UNITARIAN CHURCH, Madison, Wisconsin, 1945–51. (ABOVE)

INTERIOR, Unitarian Church, 1945–51. (OPPOSITE)

ANNUNCIATION GREEK ORTHODOX CHURCH, Wauwatosa, Wisconsin, 1955–61. (PAGE 112)

INTERIOR, William Palmer House, 1950. (ABOVE)

WILLIAM PALMER HOUSE, Ann Arbor, Michigan, 1950. (LEFT)

SOL FRIEDMAN HOUSE, TOYHILL, Pleasantville,
New York, 1948. (RIGHT)

ROLAND REISLEY HOUSE, Pleasantville, New York, 1951.
(BELOW)

H. C. PRICE COMPANY TOWER,
Bartlesville, Oklahoma, 1952–56. (LEFT)

SIDE CHAIR, H. C. Price Company Tower, c. 1956. Aluminum with upholstered seat and back, $32^5/_8 \times 19 \times 20^3/_4$ in. (82.9 × 48.3 × 52.7 cm). (ABOVE)

BETH SHOLOM SYNAGOGUE, Elkins Park, Pennsylvania, 1953–59. (ABOVE)

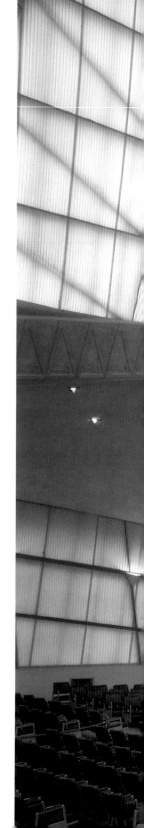

INTERIOR, Beth Sholom Synagogue, 1953–59. (RIGHT)

WILLIAM TRACY HOUSE, Normandy Park, Washington, 1955. (ABOVE)

WILLIAM TRACY HOUSE, 1955. (OPPOSITE)

THE MILE HIGH ILLINOIS, Chicago, 1956; unbuilt. Perspective.

SOLOMON R. GUGGENHEIM MUSEUM, New York, 1943–59. (OPPOSITE)

INTERIOR, Solomon R. Guggenheim Museum, 1943–59. (BELOW)

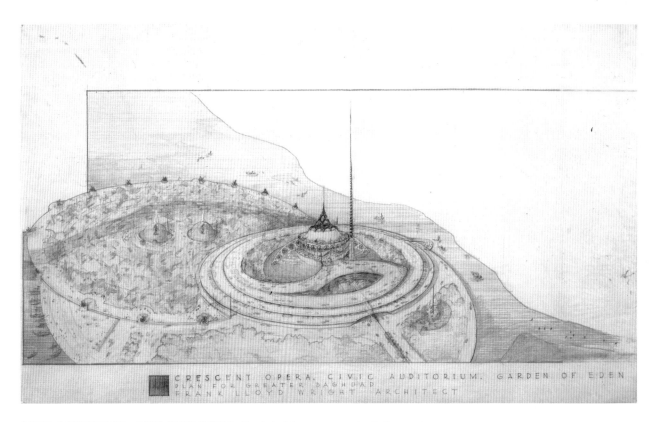

CIVIC AUDITORIUM, CRESCENT OPERA, Baghdad, Iraq, 1957; unbuilt. Perspective. (ABOVE)

FABRIC (DESIGN NO. 104) for F. Schumacher & Co., New York, 1955. Printed silk and Fortisan, 117³/₈ × 49³/₄ in. (298 × 126.4 cm). (LEFT)

INTERIOR, Solomon R. Guggenheim Museum, 1943–59. (OPPOSITE)

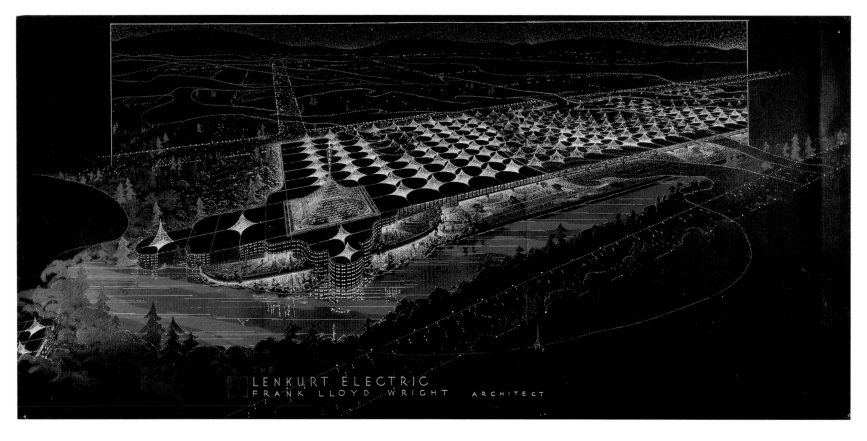

LENKURT ELECTRIC COMPANY, San Mateo, California, 1955; unbuilt. Perspective.
(ABOVE)

ARIZONA STATE CAPITOL, OASIS, Phoenix, 1957; unbuilt. Perspective. (RIGHT)

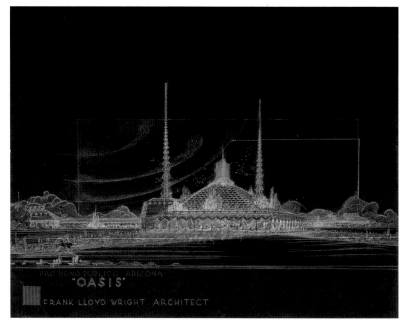

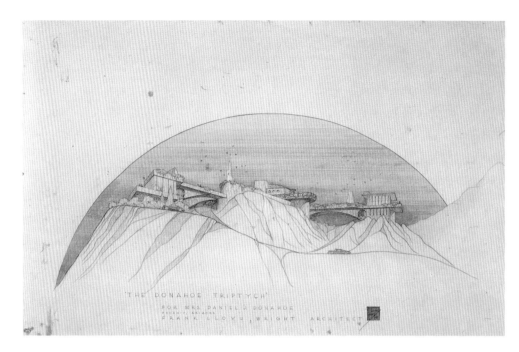

HELEN DONAHOE HOUSE, THE DONAHOE TRIPTYCH,
Paradise Valley, Arizona, 1959; unbuilt. Perspective. (RIGHT)

NORMAN LYKES HOUSE, Phoenix, Arizona, 1959–66. (BELOW)

MARIN COUNTY CIVIC CENTER, San Rafael, California, 1957–62.

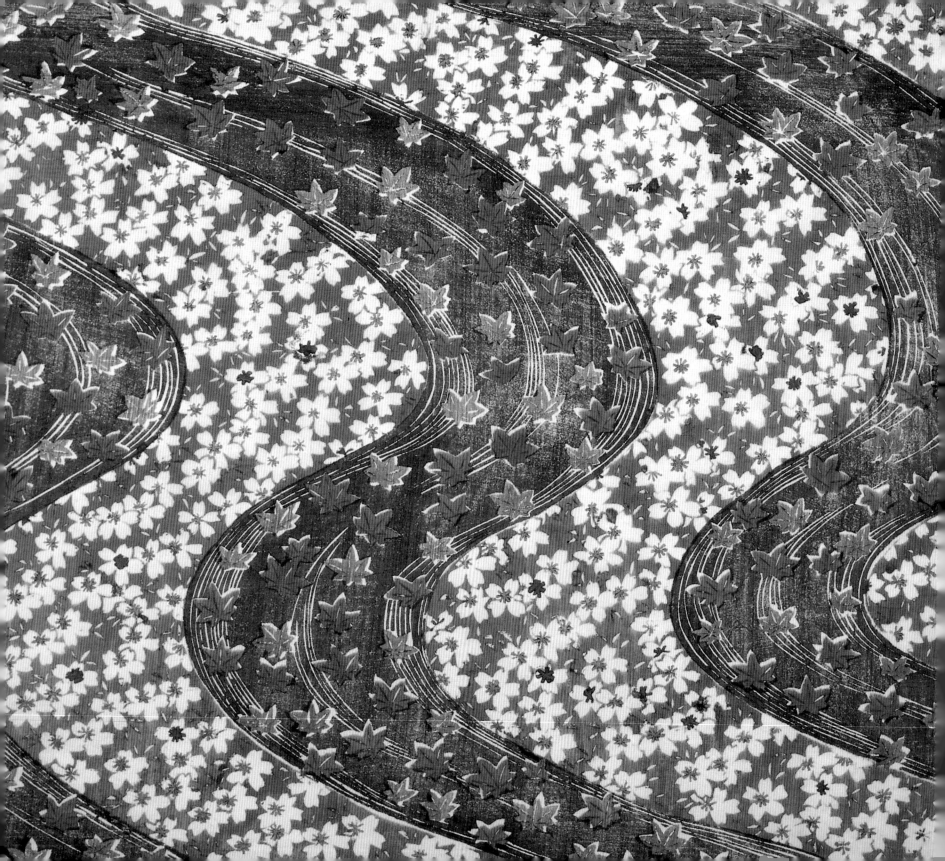

WRIGHT'S ART COLLECTION

Broadly stated . . . , the first and supreme principle of Japanese aesthetics consists in stringent simplification by elimination of the insignificant and a consequent emphasis of reality.

Wright, THE JAPANESE PRINT: AN INTERPRETATION, 1912

In explaining why the Guggenheim Museum is not well suited for the display of certain works of twentieth-century painting and sculpture, it has been argued that Wright did not care for art. Nothing could be farther from the truth. For over sixty years, up to his death in 1959, Wright was consumed by a passion for Asian art. At different periods in his life, he was an eager student, an avid collector, a discerning connoisseur, a recognized authority, an enterprising dealer, and a patient teacher. By the middle of the 1920s, he had amassed thousands of objects ranging from Japanese wood block prints (*ukiyo-e* and *surimono;* see below), screens, kakemonos, textiles, ceramics, printed papers, Chinese bronzes, sculpture, and rugs. A more startling statistic would be the number—probably in the tens of thousands—of art objects (primarily *ukiyo-e*) that he once possessed but then gave up, as they were sold at auction or to collectors to repay loans, were destroyed by the two fires at Taliesin, or were given away as collateral for loans or as outright gifts.

Wright may have begun collecting Asian art even before the turn of the century. It was during the Prairie period that he inaugurated a pattern he maintained for the remainder of his life. One part of his collection was always on view, carefully integrated into his living environment with rugs on the floor; textiles draped over chairs and pianos; ceramics, sculpture, and lacquer ware on top of bookcases and tables. Later, at Taliesin and Taliesin West (Wright's winter retreat in Arizona), he also built certain objects—Japanese screens and Chinese sculpture—directly into the architecture. The other part of his collection remained in storage—primarily fragile works on paper such as *ukiyo-e* and *surimono*—for the purpose of conservation. Periodically, these objects would be brought out to illustrate a talk on aesthetics or to be rotated among several print stands that Wright designed especially for their temporary display.

Wright not only collected art, but he lived in intimate contact with it. As a result, it is not difficult to reason that, as well as deriving aesthetic joy from his art collection, he found that it also had meaning. Asian art reflected the Eastern point of view, shared by Wright, that man should act in harmony with nature, rather than dominate it, as is the Western attitude. In Eastern thought, nature is more than a catalogue of physical specimens of flora and fauna, it is the manifestation of a cosmic order (of which man is a part) that gives spiritual unity to the universe. That unity is expressed in the geometric forms of natural elements that comprise so much of the subject matter of Asian art. Wright had absorbed these ideas as a boy from the Transcendentalist writers, especially Ralph Waldo Emerson; but works of Asian art gave these ideas physical form.

UKIYO-E. Japanese color woodcuts that depict subjects of everyday life such as portraits of actors or famous scenes from plays, celebrated landscapes, or courtesans. As a popular art, *ukiyo-e* were produced in large editions.

SURIMONO. Color woodcuts that were commissioned by groups of amateur poets for special occasions. *Surimono* illustrate a poem that appears along with the image and as such represent a collaboration of poet and artist. They were privately printed in limited editions and are considered more rare than *ukiyo-e.*

CHIYOGAMI. Sheets of decorative papers that are used for wrapping a variety of objects including books, boxes, and gifts. Prior to the late nineteenth century, they were hand-printed using wood blocks and employed images from the natural world emblematic of themes such as longevity, or as in the case of the motif, *genji-ko,* a symbolic pattern derived from an element that appears in the literary classic, *The Tale of Genji.*

Studio of Kano Motonobu (1476–1559). **THE FOUR ACCOMPLISHMENTS,** late 16th to early 17th century (Muromachi
   Period). Ink and color on paper, 65³/₄ × 101³/₈ (167 × 358 cm). (ABOVE)

Detail of **CHERRY BLOSSOMS AND MAPLE LEAVES ON FLOATING WATER** (chiyogami), c. 1850s (Late Edo Period).
   Woodcut, 13³/₈ × 18¹/₂ in. (34 × 47 cm). (PAGE 132)

Seal of Kano Jinnojō (active late 16th century). **THE MUSIC PERFORMANCE** from **THE TALE OF GENJI,** c. 1600. Ink, color, and gold leaf on paper, 67³/₄ × 146½ in. (172 × 372 cm).

Andō Hiroshige (1797–1858). **ROUGH SEA AT NARUTO IN AWA PROVINCE** from the series **PICTURES OF FAMOUS PLACES IN THE SIXTY-ODD PROVINCES, NO. 55,** 1855. Woodcut, 9⅝ × 9 in. (24.5 × 23 cm).

Andō Hiroshige (1797–1858). **THE PLUM ORCHARD AT KAMEIDO** from **ONE HUNDRED VIEWS OF FAMOUS PLACES IN EDO, NO. 30,** 1857. Woodcut, $9^{5}/_{8}$ × 9 in (24.5 × 23 cm).

Katsushika Hokusai (1760–1849). **HOBBY HORSE** from **THE HORSE SERIES**
(surimono), 1822. Woodcut, 8⅜ × 7½ in. (21.2 × 19 cm).

Katsushika Hokusai (1760–1849). **COLTS OF THE SHŌGI BOARD** from **THE
HORSE SERIES** (surimono), 1822. Woodcut, 8⅜ × 7⅜ in. (21.2 × 18.6 cm).

Katsukawa Shuntei (1770–1820). **A WOMAN WITH A CHINESE FAN AND TWO CHILDREN** from the series **SEVEN WOMEN AS THE GODS OF GOOD LUCK** (surimono), c. 1825. Woodcut, 8 × 7¼ in. (20.4 × 18.4 cm).

Ryūryūkyo Shinsai (active c. late 1780s–early 1820s). **A PORCELAIN EWER, FOOD SERVER, AND CUPS** (surimono), c. 1820. Woodcut, 7⅞ × 7¼ in. (20.1 × 18.3 cm).

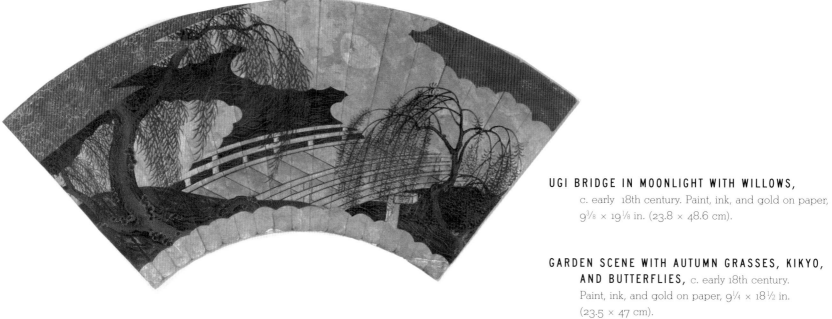

UGI BRIDGE IN MOONLIGHT WITH WILLOWS,
c. early 18th century. Paint, ink, and gold on paper,
9⅜ × 19⅛ in. (23.8 × 48.6 cm).

**GARDEN SCENE WITH AUTUMN GRASSES, KIKYO,
AND BUTTERFLIES,** c. early 18th century.
Paint, ink, and gold on paper, 9¼ × 18½ in.
(23.5 × 47 cm).

CHRONOLOGY

1867   June 8. Born in Richland Center, Wisconsin.

1885   Enters University of Wisconsin, Madison, as student of civil engineering.

1887   Enters the firm of Adler and Sullivan in Chicago.

1889   Marries Catherine Lee Tobin and fathers six children over the next fourteen years.

1893   Opens independent practice.

1900   Sets forth principles of Prairie House in two articles in *Ladies' Home Journal*.

1905   Travels to Japan, his first overseas trip, and begins avidly collecting Asian art.

1909   Leaves Catherine Lee Tobin; travels to Europe accompanied by Mamah Borthwick Cheney.

1910–11   *Studies and Executed Buildings* published by Ernst Wasmuth, Berlin. Moves with Mamah Borthwick Cheney to new house and studio, Taliesin, near Spring Green, Wisconsin.

1913   Travels again to Japan to pursue commission for the Imperial Hotel in Tokyo.

1914   At Taliesin, while Wright is working in Chicago, an insane servant kills Mamah Borthwick Cheney and six others and destroys the house by fire. Wright immediately begins to rebuild Taliesin.

1916–22   Accompanied by Miriam Noel, Wright spends the majority of these years in Japan and Los Angeles, California.

1923   Opens an office in Los Angeles and invents the textile block system of concrete construction. Marries Miriam Noel.

1924   Returns permanently to Taliesin, separates from Miriam Noel; meets Olga Lazovich.

1928   Marries Olga Lazovich.

1932   Founds the Taliesin Fellowship and publishes *An Autobiography*.

1935   Exhibits model of Broadacre City.

1936   Builds the first Usonian House for Herbert and Katherine Jacobs.

1937–41   Builds winter house and studio, Taliesin West, in Paradise Valley, Arizona.

1943   Receives commission to design a museum for Solomon R. Guggenheim; it is completed in 1959.

1949   The American Institute of Architects awards Wright the Gold Medal.

1951   Revises textile block construction for Usonian Automatic. Retrospective, *Sixty Years of Living Architecture*, begins world tour.

1959   April 9. Dies in Phoenix, Arizona.

SUGGESTIONS FOR FURTHER READING

Alofsin, Anthony. FRANK LLOYD WRIGHT, THE LOST YEARS, 1910–1922: A STUDY IN INFLUENCE. Chicago: University of Chicago Press, 1993.
 The first volume of a trilogy exploring Wright's relationship with modern European architecture and art.

Bolon, Carol R., Robert S. Nelson, and Linda Siedel, eds. THE NATURE OF FRANK LLOYD WRIGHT. Chicago: University of Chicago Press, 1988.
 Contains an essay by recognized authority Julia Meech on Wright's collection of Japanese art.

Futagawa, Yukio, ed., and Bruce Brooks Pfeiffer, text. FRANK LLOYD WRIGHT. 12 vols. Tokyo: A.D.A. Edita, 1984–88.
 A comprehensive selection of color photographs and Wright drawings documenting his buildings and projects.

Gannett, William C. THE HOUSE BEAUTIFUL. San Francisco: Pomegranate, 1996.
 Centennial edition of this Wright-designed work.

Hanks, David A. THE DECORATIVE DESIGNS OF FRANK LLOYD WRIGHT. New York: Dutton, 1979.
 The best study of Wright's designs for furniture, household objects, and graphic art.

Kaufmann, jr., Edgar. FALLINGWATER: A FRANK LLOYD WRIGHT COUNTRY HOUSE. New York: Abbeville Press, 1986.
 A lavishly illustrated history and analysis by a prominent art historian and son of the clients.

Levine, Neil. THE ARCHITECTURE OF FRANK LLOYD WRIGHT. Princeton, New Jersey: Princeton University Press, 1996.
 A scholarly explication of Wright's theory of architecture.

Lipman, Jonathan. FRANK LLOYD WRIGHT AND THE JOHNSON WAX BUILDINGS. New York: Rizzoli International, 1986.
 A history of the design and construction of the Administration Building and Research Laboratory Tower.

Merviss, Joan, with John T. Carpenter. THE FRANK LLOYD WRIGHT COLLECTION OF SURIMONO. New York and Phoenix, Arizona: Weatherhill Inc. and the Phoenix Art Museum, 1995.
 Catalogue that accompanied the exhibit *Frank Lloyd Wright and Japanese Art*. Illustrated in color and black and white with important scholarly essays.

Pfeiffer, Bruce Brooks, ed. FRANK LLOYD WRIGHT: COLLECTED WRITINGS. 5 vols. New York: Rizzoli International, 1992–95.
 A comprehensive collection of published and unpublished writing including *An Autobiography*.

Quinan, Jack. FRANK LLOYD WRIGHT'S LARKIN BUILDING: MYTH AND FACT. New York: Architectural History Foundation, 1987.
 A history of the design of and critical reaction to Wright's first major public building.

Riley, Terence, ed. FRANK LLOYD WRIGHT: ARCHITECT. New York: Museum of Modern Art, 1994.
 The catalogue for the largest Wright exhibit ever held, with several insightful scholarly essays.

Secrest, Meryle. FRANK LLOYD WRIGHT. New York: Knopf, 1992.
 The best biography to date.

Sergeant, John. FRANK LLOYD WRIGHT'S USONIAN HOUSES: A CASE FOR ORGANIC ARCHITECTURE. New York: Whitney Library of Design, Watson-Guptill, 1976.
 Documentation and analysis of the theory, design, and construction system of Usonian Houses.

Frank Lloyd Wright (LEFT) and associates in Japan, c. 1920.

Smith, Kathryn. **FRANK LLOYD WRIGHT, HOLLY-HOCK HOUSE, AND OLIVE HILL: BUILDINGS AND PROJECTS FOR ALINE BARNSDALL.** New York: Rizzoli International, 1992.

Documentation, history, and analysis of one of Wright's largest commissions (1914–24).

Storrer, William Allin. **THE FRANK LLOYD WRIGHT COMPANION.** Chicago: University of Chicago Press, 1993.

An illustrated compendium with addresses of every building Wright designed.

Sweeney, Robert L. **WRIGHT IN HOLLYWOOD: VISIONS OF A NEW ARCHITECTURE.** New York: Architectural History Foundation, 1994.

A study of Wright's textile block system of concrete construction (1923–32).